# SCRAPPER'S Best Friend

volume two

Compiled by
Melody Ross

# Table of Contents

| | |
|---|---|
| Introduction | 3 |
| How to use your new Scrapbooker's Best Friend™ | 4 |
| Accomplishments | 5 |
| Babies | 6, 7 |
| Brainstormers | 8, 9 |
| Bad Hair Days | 10, 11 |
| Celebrations | 12 |
| Christmas | 13 |
| Death & Dying | 14, 15 |
| Fathers | 16 |
| Family | 17 |
| Friendships | 18 |
| Grandparents | 19, 20 |
| Inspirations | 21 |
| Kids do the funniest things! | 22–24 |
| Mothers | 25 |
| Old Folks | 26, 27 |
| Parenting | 28, 29 |
| Romance | 30, 31 |
| Scrapaholics | 32 |
| Siblings | 33 |
| Title Pages | 34, 35 |
| Traveling | 36 |
| When I was your age | 37 |
| Words of Wisdom | 38 |
| Work | 39 |

# Introduction

There's nothing more fun than looking through a scrapbook . . . especially when it tells the story of someone who has gone before us. The memories and legacy that we leave behind are our most precious gifts to future generations. It is with these thoughts that we present volume two to you! While these phrases will add a wonderful touch to your pages, the most important part of your scrapbooks will be the names, dates and special feelings and memories that you record beside your pictures. These are the gifts that will inspire and touch the hearts of your future posterity. May you continue to take the time to do this selfless work, and forever be blessed for your creative endeavors!

Melody Ross, Chatterbox

# How to enjoy your new
# Scrapbooker's Best Friend™

- ♥ Pick a subject from the table of contents that best suits the picture you're going to put the phrase with.

- ♥ Choose just the right phrase to touch your heart or tickle your funny bone.

- ♥ Apply the phrase with pen or marker of your choice—we recommend the ZIG® Memory System® for best results. Or, create your phrase with a computer font.

- ♥ Remember to include names, dates, and special details!

- ♥ Keep your Scrapbooker's Best Friend™ with you everywhere you go!

Copyright ©2001 by EK Success. All rights reserved. Printed in China. Permission is hereby granted with purchase to reproduce the ideas in this book on a limited basis for personal use only. Mechanical reproduction of any part of this book for commercial gain or any reason, in any form, or by any means, in whole or in part is forbidden by law without written permission of EK Success

# Accomplishments

- ♥ Genius is 10% inspiration, 90% perspiration.
- ♥ If you don't make mistakes, you don't make anything.
- ♥ It's never to late to learn!
- ♥ Many are called, few are chosen.
- ♥ No pain, no gain!
- ♥ Slowly but surely.
- ♥ You win some, you lose some.
- ♥ A talent is both a gift and an obligation.
- ♥ Great things are expected of you!
- ♥ Life is whatever we choose to make of it!

# Babies

- ♥ Special things come in small packages.
- ♥ So many toys, so little time!
- ♥ Small is beautiful!
- ♥ A little pot is sooner hot!
- ♥ People who say they can sleep like a baby most often don't have one.
- ♥ Babies make us enter a "changing" world.
- ♥ You must have been a beautiful baby!
- ♥ You have got the cutest little baby face!
- ♥ Such a big miracle in such a little body!
- ♥ I'm rocking my babies because babies don't keep.
- ♥ Baby of mine, for such a short time, Fast passing years, my eyes full of tears.

- ♥ Sent from above, our bundle of love!
- ♥ If you thought he was proud of his car, you should see him carry around his new baby!
- ♥ Worth the wait!
- ♥ BABY ON BOARD!

## Priceless Little Parts

These little hands will grow up to be,
big and strong and helpful, you see.
These teeny-tiny little toes,
will carry this body that grows and grows.
This precious, sweet and radiant smile,
will help me go the extra mile.
And deep inside, a soul and heart,
destined to be special from the start.

# Brainstormers

- Snug as a bug in a rug.
- Like two peas in a pod.
- Bright eyed and bushy tailed.
- Finders, keepers . . .
- When it rains it pours.
- A picture is worth a thousand words.
- Busy as a bee.
- Clean as a whistle.
- As good as gold.
- Naked as a jaybird.
- Proud as a peacock.
- Quick as greased lightning.
- A penny for your thoughts.
- An apple a day keeps the doctor away.
- You're the apple of my eye!

- ♥ Variety is the spice of life
- ♥ Monkey see, monkey do!
- ♥ Life is so sweet!
- ♥ What goes up must come down!
- ♥ You scratch my back, I'll scratch yours.
- ♥ Good things come in small packages!
- ♥ Cat got your tongue?
- ♥ A penny saved is a penny earned!
- ♥ As old as the hills!
- ♥ As old as the trees!
- ♥ Here today, gone tomorrow!
- ♥ United we stand, divided we fall.
- ♥ The eyes are the window to the soul.
- ♥ There are more fish in the sea.
- ♥ Aged to perfection!

# Bad Hair Days...

- I'm having a bad hair day!
- It's got to be a blessing in disguise.
- Better late than never!
- Will this day ever end?
- I got up on the wrong side of the bed!
- When it rains, it pours!
- So many chores, so little time!
- What cannot be cured, must be endured.
- What doesn't kill us only makes us stronger.
- Laughter is the best medicine.
- Stumbling is not falling.
- It's not the end of the world, it's just the intermission.

- ♥ Different strokes for different folks.
- ♥ It takes all kinds to make a world!
- ♥ I'm nice, you can't expect me to be organized too!
- ♥ Man cannot live on stress alone!
- ♥ Some times bad days happen to good people.
- ♥ You win some, you lose some.
- ♥ It takes 17 muscles to smile and 42 muscles to frown.
- ♥ There's always tomorrow!
- ♥ Tomorrow is another day!
- ♥ When life gives you garbage, recycle it!
- ♥ TOMORROW OR BUST!

# Celebrations

- ♥ A great time was had by all!
- ♥ The more, the merrier!
- ♥ Laughter is contagious!
- ♥ Life's merry when friends meet!
- ♥ How blessed we are to have friends to party with!
- ♥ A cause for celebration!
- ♥ Happy everything!
- ♥ Happy un-birthday!
- ♥ With the right bunch of people, life can be a party!
- ♥ Congratulation celebration!
- ♥ I love a good party!
- ♥ Who needs a holiday to have a bash?

# Christmas

♥ May our Christmas cheer
last all through the year!

♥ The happiest Christmases
are heavenly Christmases.

♥ Santa stuffs stockings,
the rest of us stuff our faces!

♥ We gather around the Christmas tree, to
thank with grateful thoughts of Thee.

♥ Don't peek, don't sneak, 'til Christmas!

♥ Holiday memories warm even
the coldest of days.

♥ I love thee, Lord Jesus.

♥ Giving feels even better than receiving.

♥ Santa's little helpers . . .

# Death & Dying

- ♥ He (she) shall be greatly missed.
- ♥ While alive she (he) really lived.
- ♥ It was an honor to be part of your life.
- ♥ Loving memories comfort the pain in our hearts.
- ♥ Absence makes the heart grow fonder.
- ♥ After a storm comes a calm.
- ♥ Love without end has no end.
- ♥ Grief is lessened when shared with others.
- ♥ They that live longest must die at last.
- ♥ No coming to heaven with dry eyes.

- ♥ An honor to know such a hero.
- ♥ One thing that I know is true, nothing is harder than missing you.
- ♥ Through life you guarded us with so much love, Now our guardian angel... from Heaven above.
- ♥ Nothing is harder than the loss of someone we love, Perhaps their greater purpose is to love us from above.
- ♥ Nothing dries sooner than tears.
- ♥ The remembrance of past sorrows is a joyful learning experience.
- ♥ It's always darkest before the dawn.
- ♥ When one door shuts, another opens.

# Fathers

- A man's home is his castle.
- Man cannot live on sports alone!
- The way to a man's heart is through his stomach.
- The way to a dad's heart is with the batting of eyelashes.
- Because I'm the dad, that's why!
- You wait until your father gets home!
- A great wife, kids and health, are a man's greatest wealth!
- HIS WIFE = His bride & joy!
- Dear old dad . . .
- Like father, like son!

# Family

- Everything begins at home.
- East or west, home is best!
- Fathers make houses, Mothers make homes.
- The family that prays together, stays together.
- There's no place like home!
- Happiness is a large supportive, close family . . . in another state.
- Home, where you always find warm words on a cold day.
- The beginning of the most perfect man began in the most humble of homes.

# Friendships

♥ Great minds think alike.

♥ There's no doctor like a true friend.

♥ Perfect friends who were once perfect strangers.

♥ Friendship-the older it grows, the stronger it is.

♥ A friend in need is a friend indeed.

♥ Friend: those who've heard the worst about us, yet refuse to believe it.

♥ I'd give you the shirt off my back!

♥ Even the best of friends must part.

♥ Forever a friend without an end.

# Grandparents

- ♥ So many grandkids, so little time!

- ♥ Grandchildren are God's compensation for gray hair and wrinkles.

- ♥ Here's to grandparents, the cheapest (and best) babysitters in the world!

- ♥ Our grandchildren-our revenge on our children.

- ♥ Great joy comes in seeing our family enter another generation.

- ♥ Carry the name proudly!

- ♥ The best grandparents ever are now the best great-grandparents ever!

- ♥ For a good time and lots of treats, call 1-800-GRANDPARENTS!

# Grandparents, *continued*...

♥ Grandparents are the most precious kind of antiques.

♥ Grandparents give roots, parents give wings.

♥ Not just grandparents, but special friends, unconditionally loving from beginning to end.

Who makes us happy when we are sad?
Who do we call for when
Mom and Dad are mad?
Who do we go to for a hug and kiss, too?
Grandpa & Grandma, that's who!

# Inspirations

♥ Every cloud has a silver lining.

♥ Know thyself,
Love thyself,
Be true to thyself.

♥ Why we have trials we don't know,
These are the times that help us grow.

♥ Seeing is believing,
Believing is seeing.

♥ A thing of beauty is a joy forever.

♥ Good always wins.

♥ A city of darkness cannot put out
the tiniest light.

♥ Faith and fear cannot reside
in the same heart.

# Kids do the funniest things!

- ♥ Kids say the funniest things!
- ♥ Kids will be kids!
- ♥ Monkey see, monkey do!
- ♥ A little knowledge is a dangerous thing!
- ♥ Ask me no questions, I'll tell you no lies!
- ♥ Kids must have 9 lives!
- ♥ Accidents will happen!
- ♥ If you don't make mistakes, you don't make anything.
- ♥ Don't cry over spilled milk!
- ♥ "Because" is my favorite reason!
- ♥ What's yours is mine, what's mine is mine!

- ♥ When the cat's away,
  the mice will play.
- ♥ Boys will be boys!
- ♥ Girls will be girls!
- ♥ Patience is a virtue . . .
- ♥ Finders, keepers!
- ♥ Leave no stone unturned!
- ♥ Add insult to injury . . .
- ♥ See no evil,
  Hear no evil,
  Speak no evil.
- ♥ If you can't behave, at least be careful!
- ♥ My cup (or bath) runneth over.
- ♥ What a show-off!
- ♥ How come when you're tired,
  I'm the one who has to take a nap?

# Kids do the funniest things, continued...

- ♥ Imitation is the most sincere form of flattery.
- ♥ Well, mommy wears lipstick!
- ♥ Pretty is as pretty does.
- ♥ The BULL IN A CHINA SHOP Club
- ♥ Fingers were made before forks.
- ♥ Fingers were made before paintbrushes.
- ♥ Cleanliness is next to Godliness.
- ♥ Experience is the best teacher.
- ♥ It's not a mess, it's a work of art!
- ♥ The bigger they are, the harder they fall.
- ♥ Actions speak louder than words.
- ♥ Love letters from kids are the best kind.

# Mothers

♥ There's no job more noble
on this earth, than to care for those
whom we've given birth.

♥ Don't cry over spilled milk . . .
unless you're the mom and
you have to clean it up.

♥ Kids that are happy & in good health,
are a mother's greatest wealth.

♥ Behind every successful child is a mother.

♥ Anyone can be a mother, it is known,
But mommies are there from the start,
Until a child is grown.

♥ The hand that rocks the cradle
rules the world.

# Old Folks

- ♥ They who live the longest see the most.
- ♥ Years know more than books!
- ♥ Not quite as wise as an owl, but always a hoot.
- ♥ Life begins at 80.
- ♥ Old men (women) are twice children.
- ♥ The longer we live, the more wonders we will see.
- ♥ Old love does not rust.
- ♥ There's many a good tune played on an old fiddle.
- ♥ Happy is she whose friends were born before her.
- ♥ The first 100 years of life are the hardest.

- ♥ If you want good advice, consult an old man (woman).
- ♥ Healthy, wealthy & wisecracking.
- ♥ Old as the hills . . .
- ♥ Old as the trees . . .
- ♥ It's never too late to learn.
- ♥ An old woman's (man's) words are seldom untrue.
- ♥ The older love grows, the stronger it is.
- ♥ Even with treasures of jewels and gold, the best is a sweetheart with whom you've grown old.
- ♥ True love never grows old.
- ♥ Old folks are the most precious antiques.

# Parenting

♥ We've entered a changing world.

♥ Quit looking at me with that tone of face!

♥ A source of joy from beginning to end,
You are our children, but also our friends.

♥ You can search treasure maps,
   and oceans so deep,
My child is my diamond,
   forever I'll keep.

♥ What part of *no* don't you understand?

♥ Parents together, a team forever.

## Real Life

Once we went out to dinner,
or out dancing for fun,
but now our life has really begun.
Nothing beats the action,
of seeing your child first walk,
or say "mama" and "dada"
as he begins to talk.

♥ My child, nothing could replace,
the loving smile upon your face.

♥ One thing now we know is true,
nothing's better than being parents to you.

♥ Our dreams came true . . .
when we became parents to you.

♥ Child of God, child of mine.

# Romance

♥ There's no love like the first love.

♥ A true love is another self.

♥ Love makes the world go 'round.

♥ There's no doctor like true love.

♥ The heart's letter is read in the eyes.

♥ It takes two to tango!

♥ Marriage: the last real decision a man gets to make.

♥ Love returned is the true reward of love given.

♥ Marriages are made in heaven.

♥ The man (woman) who won my heart . . . and my mother's approval.

- ♥ Love without end has no end.
- ♥ Love will find a way.
- ♥ Marriage-one soul in two bodies.
- ♥ All's fair in love and war.
- ♥ When children find true love, parents find true joy.
- ♥ May our love be as endless as our bands of gold.
- ♥ Absence makes the heart grow fonder.
- ♥ My partner in life and in love, A partnership sealed from Heaven above, A marriage forever, without an end, Thankfully, also my very best friend.
- ♥ A true love stays when the rest of the world walks out.
- ♥ In your arms is my favorite place to be.

# Scrapaholics

- My name is _____, and I'm a scrapaholic.

- Scrappy days are here again.

- So many pictures, so little time!

- Woman cannot live on picture albums alone!

- Nothing's better than time to spend, Croppin' and talkin' with you, my friend.

- Never be tardy to a cropping party!

- To crop or not to crop, that is the question.

# Siblings

♥ Sisters (brothers) are
the best kind of friends.

♥ My brother, my buddy . . .

♥ My sister, my friend . . .

♥ Of all the things that I have to play,
I'd choose my sister (brother) any day!

♥ Am I my brothers keeper?

♥ First a bother,
then a brother,
now a friend.

♥ When I count my blessings,
the greatest of my joys,
Our parents gave us siblings,
instead of rooms of toys.

# Title pages

- ♥ Our Loving Legacies
- ♥ Our Very Special Memories
- ♥ Family Good Times
- ♥ Fond Memories of Family & Friends
- ♥ Our Book of Heritage
- ♥ Fantastically Fun Family Times
- ♥ Our Big Book of Family Trips
- ♥ The Days of Our Lives
- ♥ The 19__ (20__) Yearbook
- ♥ Marvelous, Magnificent Memories

- ♥ The Book of Most Beautiful Babies
- ♥ All About the Special Girl, Who Brings Happiness Into Our World.
- ♥ All About the Special Boy, Who Fills Our Lives With So Much Joy.
- ♥ The Most Special Day Ever
- ♥ The Best Day Of 19__ (20__)
- ♥ The Story of a Champion
- ♥ The Story of a Silent Hero
- ♥ The Roots That Gave Us Our Wings
- ♥ The Day That Two Became One.

# Traveling

- Bon voyage!

- Travel broadens the mind . . .
  and often the waistline.

- He travels fastest who travels alone,
  he travels happiest who travels
  with his family.

- Seeing the world and with it,
     falling in love,
  Is seeing the creation,
     and what God is capable of.

- Destination Relaxation!

- The trip of a lifetime!

- The world is a beautiful place!

- The world doesn't stand still!

# When I was your age . . .

When I was your age, bread was a penny,
We worked for hours for just a little money.
Kids were just seen and never were heard,
the best kind of kids from what I have heard.
We walked to school for long miles at a time,
Ate a year of school lunches for only a dime.
Each night from the Bible,
We'd recite a whole page,
And listen to Grandpa say,
"When I was your age . . ."

♥ We had to walk 10 miles to school in the snow, uphill, both ways.

♥ Life was slower back then.

# Words of Wisdom

♥ He who laughs, lasts.

♥ The best things in life are not free, but priceless.

♥ Do unto others as you would have others do unto you.

♥ The more things change, the more they stay the same.

♥ There's a time and a place for everything. . . it's always time for happiness.

♥ A man should look for what he is, and not what he thinks he should be.

♥ With God, anything is possible.

# Work

♥ Who invented work, anyway?

♥ A little hard work never hurt anyone!

♥ Happiness comes from work well done.

♥ Whistle while you work!

♥ Put your shoulder to the wheel!

♥ The best way to kill time is to work it to death.

♥ All play and no work. . .

♥ Business before pleasure. . .

♥ Many hands make light work.

♥ All work and no pay—
that's what you call housework!